© 2019 Ryan Morgan
Cover by Ryan Morgan. Images from Vecteezy and Unsplash.

# CONTENTS

RESEARCH

PLACES TO GO

_____
_____
_____
_____
_____
_____
_____
_____
_____

PLACES TO EAT

_____
_____
_____
_____
_____
_____
_____
_____

 # RESEARCH

THINGS TO DO

NOTES

TRAVEL CALENDAR

MONTH: ....

SUN	MON	TUE	WED	THU	FRI	SAT

Notes:

_____

_____

_____

_____

TRAVEL CALENDAR

MONTH: ....

SUN	MON	TUE	WED	THU	FRI	SAT

Notes:

_____

_____

_____

_____

# RESERVATIONS

DESTINATION: ....

Flight:	Confirmation #:
Airport:	Departing:
Airline:	Arriving:

Flight:	Confirmation #:
Airport:	Departing:
Airline:	Arriving:

Rental Car:	Confirmation #:
Rental Company:	
Pick Up:	Drop Off:

Lodging:	Confirmation #:
Check In:	Address:
Check Out:	

Notes:

_____

_____

_____

_____

 RESERVATIONS

DESTINATION: ....

Flight:	Confirmation #:
Airport:	Departing:
Airline:	Arriving:

Flight:	Confirmation #:
Airport:	Departing:
Airline:	Arriving:

Rental Car:	Confirmation #:
Rental Company:	
Pick Up:	Drop Off:

Lodging:	Confirmation #:
Check In:	Address:
Check Out:	

Notes:

_____

_____

_____

_____

TRAVEL BUDGET

EXPENSE	BUDGET	ACTUAL

⚑ TRAVEL BUDGET

EXPENSE	BUDGET	ACTUAL

PACKING LIST

ITEM	☑

PACKING LIST

ITEM	☑

ITINERARY

DATE: ....

SCHEDULE	
5:00 AM	
6:00 AM	
7:00 AM	
8:00 AM	
9:00 AM	
10:00 AM	
11:00 AM	
12:00 PM	
1:00 PM	
2:00 PM	
3:00 PM	
4:00 PM	
5:00 PM	
6:00 PM	
7:00 PM	
8:00 PM	
9:00 PM	
10:00 PM	
11:00 PM	
12:00 PM	

MEALS

BREAKFAST:

LUNCH:

DINNER:

ACTIVITIES

NOTES

MEMORIES

DATE: ....

ITINERARY

DATE: ....

SCHEDULE	
5:00 AM	
6:00 AM	
7:00 AM	
8:00 AM	
9:00 AM	
10:00 AM	
11:00 AM	
12:00 PM	
1:00 PM	
2:00 PM	
3:00 PM	
4:00 PM	
5:00 PM	
6:00 PM	
7:00 PM	
8:00 PM	
9:00 PM	
10:00 PM	
11:00 PM	
12:00 PM	

MEALS

BREAKFAST:

LUNCH:

DINNER:

ACTIVITIES

NOTES

MEMORIES

DATE: ....

ITINERARY   DATE: ....

SCHEDULE	
5:00 AM	
6:00 AM	
7:00 AM	
8:00 AM	
9:00 AM	
10:00 AM	
11:00 AM	
12:00 PM	
1:00 PM	
2:00 PM	
3:00 PM	
4:00 PM	
5:00 PM	
6:00 PM	
7:00 PM	
8:00 PM	
9:00 PM	
10:00 PM	
11:00 PM	
12:00 PM	

MEALS

BREAKFAST:

LUNCH:

DINNER:

ACTIVITIES

NOTES

MEMORIES

DATE: ....

ITINERARY

DATE: ....

SCHEDULE	
5:00 AM	
6:00 AM	
7:00 AM	
8:00 AM	
9:00 AM	
10:00 AM	
11:00 AM	
12:00 PM	
1:00 PM	
2:00 PM	
3:00 PM	
4:00 PM	
5:00 PM	
6:00 PM	
7:00 PM	
8:00 PM	
9:00 PM	
10:00 PM	
11:00 PM	
12:00 PM	

MEALS

BREAKFAST:

LUNCH:

DINNER:

ACTIVITIES

NOTES

MEMORIES

DATE: ....

ITINERARY

DATE: ....

SCHEDULE	
5:00 AM	
6:00 AM	
7:00 AM	
8:00 AM	
9:00 AM	
10:00 AM	
11:00 AM	
12:00 PM	
1:00 PM	
2:00 PM	
3:00 PM	
4:00 PM	
5:00 PM	
6:00 PM	
7:00 PM	
8:00 PM	
9:00 PM	
10:00 PM	
11:00 PM	
12:00 PM	

MEALS

BREAKFAST:

LUNCH:

DINNER:

ACTIVITIES

NOTES

MEMORIES

DATE: ....

ITINERARY

DATE: ....

SCHEDULE	
5:00 AM	
6:00 AM	
7:00 AM	
8:00 AM	
9:00 AM	
10:00 AM	
11:00 AM	
12:00 PM	
1:00 PM	
2:00 PM	
3:00 PM	
4:00 PM	
5:00 PM	
6:00 PM	
7:00 PM	
8:00 PM	
9:00 PM	
10:00 PM	
11:00 PM	
12:00 PM	

MEALS

BREAKFAST:

LUNCH:

DINNER:

ACTIVITIES

NOTES

MEMORIES

ITINERARY

DATE: ....

SCHEDULE	
5:00 AM	
6:00 AM	
7:00 AM	
8:00 AM	
9:00 AM	
10:00 AM	
11:00 AM	
12:00 PM	
1:00 PM	
2:00 PM	
3:00 PM	
4:00 PM	
5:00 PM	
6:00 PM	
7:00 PM	
8:00 PM	
9:00 PM	
10:00 PM	
11:00 PM	
12:00 PM	

MEALS

BREAKFAST:

LUNCH:

DINNER:

ACTIVITIES

NOTES

MEMORIES

DATE: ....

ITINERARY

DATE: ....

SCHEDULE	
5:00AM	
6:00AM	
7:00AM	
8:00AM	
9:00AM	
10:00AM	
11:00AM	
12:00PM	
1:00PM	
2:00PM	
3:00PM	
4:00PM	
5:00PM	
6:00PM	
7:00PM	
8:00PM	
9:00PM	
10:00PM	
11:00PM	
12:00PM	

MEALS

BREAKFAST:

LUNCH:

DINNER:

ACTIVITIES

NOTES

MEMORIES

ITINERARY

DATE: ....

SCHEDULE	
5:00 AM	
6:00 AM	
7:00 AM	
8:00 AM	
9:00 AM	
10:00 AM	
11:00 AM	
12:00 PM	
1:00 PM	
2:00 PM	
3:00 PM	
4:00 PM	
5:00 PM	
6:00 PM	
7:00 PM	
8:00 PM	
9:00 PM	
10:00 PM	
11:00 PM	
12:00 PM	

MEALS

BREAKFAST:

LUNCH:

DINNER:

ACTIVITIES

NOTES

MEMORIES

DATE:

ITINERARY

DATE: ....

SCHEDULE	
5:00AM	
6:00AM	
7:00AM	
8:00AM	
9:00AM	
10:00AM	
11:00AM	
12:00PM	
1:00PM	
2:00PM	
3:00PM	
4:00PM	
5:00PM	
6:00PM	
7:00PM	
8:00PM	
9:00PM	
10:00PM	
11:00PM	
12:00PM	

MEALS

BREAKFAST:

LUNCH:

DINNER:

ACTIVITIES

NOTES

MEMORIES

DATE: ....

ITINERARY

DATE: ....

SCHEDULE	
5:00 AM	
6:00 AM	
7:00 AM	
8:00 AM	
9:00 AM	
10:00 AM	
11:00 AM	
12:00 PM	
1:00 PM	
2:00 PM	
3:00 PM	
4:00 PM	
5:00 PM	
6:00 PM	
7:00 PM	
8:00 PM	
9:00 PM	
10:00 PM	
11:00 PM	
12:00 PM	

MEALS

BREAKFAST:

LUNCH:

DINNER:

ACTIVITIES

NOTES

MEMORIES

ITINERARY   DATE: ....

SCHEDULE	
5:00 AM	
6:00 AM	
7:00 AM	
8:00 AM	
9:00 AM	
10:00 AM	
11:00 AM	
12:00 PM	
1:00 PM	
2:00 PM	
3:00 PM	
4:00 PM	
5:00 PM	
6:00 PM	
7:00 PM	
8:00 PM	
9:00 PM	
10:00 PM	
11:00 PM	
12:00 PM	

MEALS

BREAKFAST:

LUNCH:

DINNER:

ACTIVITIES

NOTES

MEMORIES

ITINERARY

DATE: ....

SCHEDULE	
5:00 AM	
6:00 AM	
7:00 AM	
8:00 AM	
9:00 AM	
10:00 AM	
11:00 AM	
12:00 PM	
1:00 PM	
2:00 PM	
3:00 PM	
4:00 PM	
5:00 PM	
6:00 PM	
7:00 PM	
8:00 PM	
9:00 PM	
10:00 PM	
11:00 PM	
12:00 PM	

MEALS

BREAKFAST:

LUNCH:

DINNER:

ACTIVITIES

NOTES

MEMORIES

DATE: ....

ITINERARY   DATE: ....

SCHEDULE	
5:00AM	
6:00AM	
7:00AM	
8:00AM	
9:00AM	
10:00AM	
11:00AM	
12:00PM	
1:00PM	
2:00PM	
3:00PM	
4:00PM	
5:00PM	
6:00PM	
7:00PM	
8:00PM	
9:00PM	
10:00PM	
11:00PM	
12:00PM	

MEALS

BREAKFAST:

LUNCH:

DINNER:

ACTIVITIES

NOTES

MEMORIES

DATE: ....

TRAVEL NOTES

TRAVEL NOTES

TRAVEL NOTES

 TRAVEL NOTES

 TRAVEL NOTES

⚑ TRAVEL NOTES

TRAVEL NOTES

⚑ TRAVEL NOTES

⚑ TRAVEL NOTES

▱ TRAVEL NOTES

TRAVEL NOTES

TRAVEL NOTES

TRAVEL NOTES

TRAVEL NOTES

TRAVEL NOTES

TRAVEL NOTES

TRAVEL NOTES

TRAVEL NOTES

TRAVEL NOTES

TRAVEL NOTES

TRAVEL NOTES

TRAVEL NOTES

Made in the USA
Middletown, DE
17 May 2025

75687030R00035